Guess Who
Hides

Adivina quién
se esconde

Sharon Gordon

Marshall Cavendish
Benchmark
New York

Splash!

I go into the pond.

It is too hot to sit in the sun.

❖

¡Paf!

Me zambullo en el estanque.

Hace mucho calor como
para sentarme al sol.

I swim to the muddy bottom.

———————❖—————

Nado hacia el fondo
enlodado.

I find my favorite food
here.
I eat plants, insects, and
fish.

———————◆———————

Aquí encuentro mi comida
favorita.

Como plantas, insectos y
peces.

I also eat dead animals.

This helps keep the pond clean.

---❖---

También como animales muertos y así ayudo a mantener limpio el estanque.

I have large eyes to see.

I do not have teeth.

❖

Tengo ojos grandes para ver
y no tengo dientes.

I do not need any.

I can bite hard with my jaw.

Pero no los necesito.

Puedo morder fuertemente con mi mandíbula.

I lay my eggs in the sand.

I dig a hole with my back legs.

❖

Cavo un hueco con mis patas y pongo mis huevos en la arena.

The eggs hatch in about 60 days.

The *hatchlings* hurry to the water.

———❖———

Los huevos tardan en incubar unos 60 días.

Las *crías* corren hacia el agua.

I do not have bones inside my body.

I have a hard shell on the outside.

❖

No tengo huesos en mi cuerpo.

Tengo un caparazón duro por fuera.

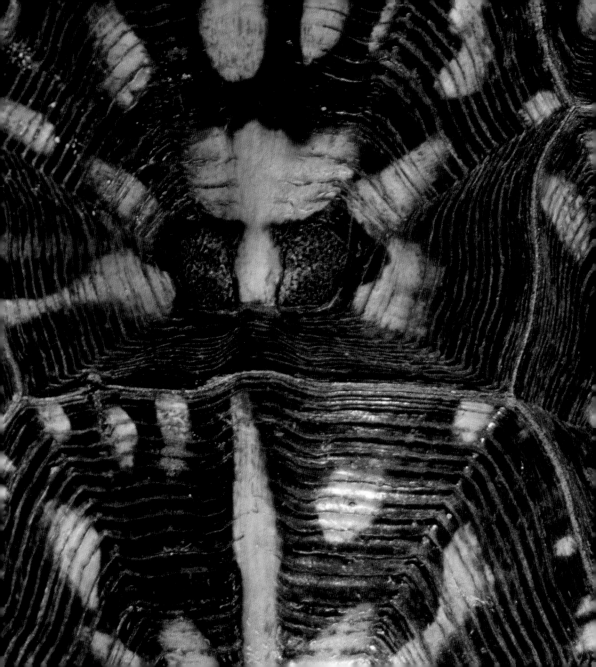

My shell is my home.

It is a great place to hide.

❖

Mi caparazón es mi hogar.

Es un buen sitio para esconderse.

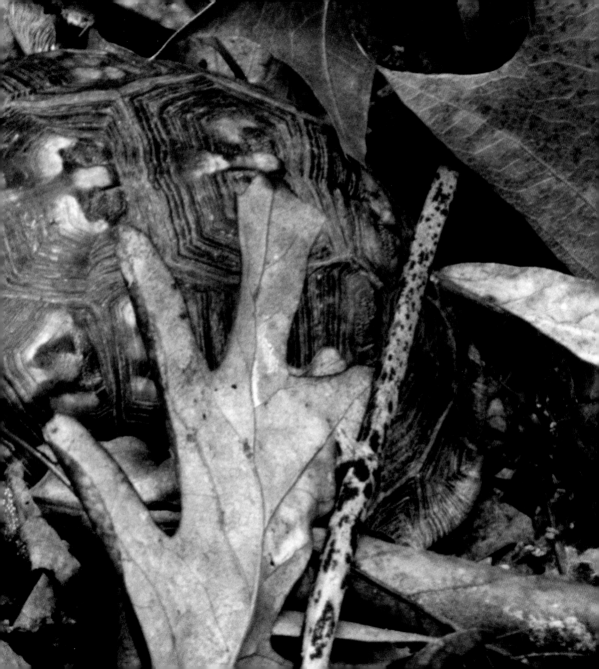

I pull in my arms, legs, and head.

Try to get me now!

———————❖———————

Yo escondo mis brazos, patas y cabeza.

¡A ver cómo me atrapas ahora!

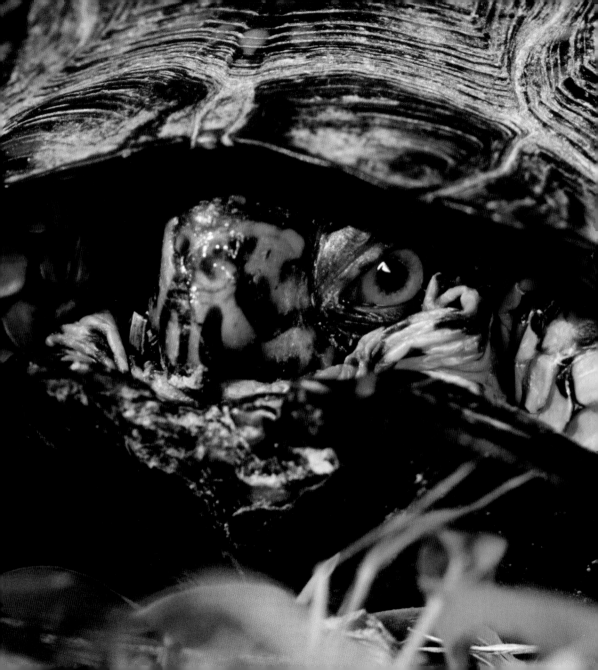

My shell is heavy.

I move slowly.

Who am I?

❖

Mi caparazón es pesado.

Por eso me muevo despacio.

¿Quién soy?

I am a turtle!

———————◆———————

¡Soy una tortuga!

Who am I?

¿Quién soy?

egg
huevo

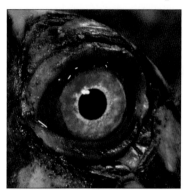

eye
ojo

hatchling
cría

jaw
mandíbula

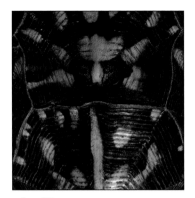

shell
caparazón

Challenge Words

Palabras avanzadas

hatchling A baby turtle that has just hatched, or broken out of its egg.

cría Una tortuguita que acaba de nacer o de salir del huevo.

29

Index

Índice

About the Author
Datos biográficos de la autora

Sharon Gordon has written many books for young children. She has always worked as an editor. Sharon and her husband Bruce have three children, Douglas, Katie, and Laura, and one spoiled pooch, Samantha. They live in Midland Park, New Jersey.

Sharon Gordon ha escrito muchos libros para niños. Siempre ha trabajado como editora. Sharon y su esposo Bruce tienen tres niños, Douglas, Katie y Laura, y una perra consentida, Samantha. Viven en Midland Park, Nueva Jersey.

With thanks to Nanci Vargus, Ed.D. and Beth Walker Gambro, reading consultants

Marshall Cavendish Benchmark
99 White Plains Road
Tarrytown, New York 10591-9001
www.marshallcavendish.us

Library of Congress Cataloging-in-Publication Data

Gordon, Sharon.
[Guess who hides. Spanish & English]
Guess who hides = Adivina quién se esconde / Sharon Gordon. — Bilingual ed.
p. cm. — (Bookworms. Guess who? = Adivina quién)
Includes index.
ISBN-13: 978-0-7614-2465-9 (bilingual edition)
ISBN-10: 0-7614-2465-2 (bilingual edition)
ISBN-13: 978-0-7614-2385-0 (Spanish edition)
ISBN-10: 0-7614-1555-6 (English edition)
1. Turtles—Juvenile literature. I. Title. II. Title: Adivina quién se esconde. III. Series: Gordon, Sharon. Bookworms.
Guess who? (Spanish & English)

QL666.C5G6718 2006b
597.92—dc22
2006016815

Spanish Translation and Text Composition by Victory Productions, Inc.
www.victoryprd.com

Photo Research by Anne Burns Images

Cover Photo by: *Corbis*/Joe McDonald

The photographs in this book are used with the permission and through the courtesy of: *Corbis*: pp. 1, 23, 27
Lynda Richardson; p. 5 Corbis; pp. 11, 15, 25, 28 (upper left and right) Joe McDonald; pp. 13, 29 (left)
David Northcott; pp. 19, 29 (right) Mary Ann McDonald; p. 21 Gary Carter. *Animals, Animals*: p. 3 E.R. Degginger.
Visuals Unlimited: p. 7 Jim Merli; p. 9 Warren Stone; pp. 17, 30 (lower) Joe McDonald.

Series design by Becky Terhune

Printed in Malaysia
1 3 5 6 4 2